COLLABORATIONS:
ENGLISH IN OUR LIVES

BEGINNING 1 WORKBOOK

Jann Huizenga

Heinle & Heinle Publishers
A Division of International Thomson Publishing, Inc.
Boston, MA 02116, U.S.A.

 The ITP logo is a trademark under license.

The publication of *Collaborations* was directed by the members of the Heinle & Heinle
Secondary and Adult ESL Publishing Team:

Publisher: Stanley Galek
Editorial Director: Roseanne Mendoza
Production Services Coordinator: Lisa McLaughlin
Market Development Director: Elaine Uzan Leary

Also participating in the publication of the program were:

Director of Production: Elizabeth Holthaus
Assistant Editor: Ann Keefe
Manufacturing Coordinator: Mary Beth Hennebury
Full Service Design and Production: PC&F, Inc.
Illustration Program: Brian Karas and PC&F, Inc.

Manufactured in the United States of America.

ISBN: 0-8384-4115-7

Heinle & Heinle is a division of International Thomson Publishing, Inc.

Photo Credits
Cover: Mark Neyndorff
Unit 1: FPG, 1; Jann Huizenga, 2, 5, 6; Mark Neyndorff, 7, 8; Sarah Hoskins, 9;
Helen Gittings, 12.
Unit 2: FPG, 17; Jann Huizenga, 18, 22; Sarah Hoskins, 21, 24.
Unit 3: James Higgins, 31, 32; Jann Huizenga, 34 top, 34 bottom, 36, 39, 42; David Plakke,
34 middle; Ziqiang Shr, 38.
Unit 4: Nancy Hunter Warren, 45; Jann Huizenga, 46, 48, 54 right, 55; Julie Graber, 50;
James Higgins, 53; Ken Light, 54 left.
Unit 5: FPG, 59; Jann Huizenga, 60, 63, 68 top left, 68 top right; 68 bottom left, 69 top,
69 bottom; Alan Malschick, 68 bottom right, 69 middle.
Unit 6: Marcus Tate, 73; Dolly Huizenga 75, 76; Peter Lee, 82.

Also, special thanks to Children's Book Press and Carmen Lomas Garza for permission to
reproduce the illustration on p. 33.

BRIEF CONTENTS ● ● ●

Unit 1 **Learning about Each Other** in San Diego   **1**

Unit 2 **Helping Each Other Learn** in Chicago   **17**

Unit 3 **No Place Like Home:** Stories from Massachusetts   **31**

Unit 4 **Working Hard** in the Southwest   **45**

Unit 5 **Familiar Faces and Places** in Miami   **59**

Unit 6 **Celebrating Together** in Cerritos, California   **73**

About This Workbook

The *Collaborations Beginning 1 Workbook* accompanies the *Collaborations Beginning 1 Student Book*. This workbook is designed to reinforce the vocabulary, lifeskills, grammar, reading skills, and writing skills from the student book. Each unit opens with a list of page numbers from the student book correlated to those in the workbook unit. This serves as a guide to students and instructors. Because the workbook is designed for self-study situations, it can be used in the classroom by students working with the instructor or by students working independently.

CONTENTS ...

About This Workbook iii

Unit 1   **Learning about Each Other in San Diego** 1

Grammar Review: The Verb *Be* 2
Doing It in English: Recognizing the Numbers 1 to 100 3
Doing It in English: Writing the Numbers 1 to 100 4
Grammar Review: Making Sentences with *Be* 5
Doing It in English: Asking and Answering Personal Questions 6
Doing It in English: Filling Out a Form 7
Grammar Review: *There Is* and *There Are* 8
Grammar Review: Noun Plurals 9
Vocabulary Review: Things You Like to Do 10
More Reading and Writing: More about Phuong Viet Duo 12
Test Yourself 15
Language Learning Diary 16

Unit 2   **Helping Each Other Learn in Chicago** 17

Grammar Review: *Like* + Infinitive 18
Grammar Review: *Always, Often, Sometimes, Never* 19
Vocabulary Review: Classroom Verbs 20
Vocabulary Review: Classroom Objects 21
Doing It in English: Reading School Signs 22
Doing It in English: Finding Your Way Around School 23
More Reading and Writing: More about Adam Czerw 24
Doing It in English: Asking Questions in Class 26
Test Yourself 29
Language Learning Diary 30

Unit 3   **No Place Like Home: Stories from Massachusetts** 31

Vocabulary Review: Verbs 32
Vocabulary Review: Family Words 33
Grammar Review: Using *In* and *On* with Place Names 34
Doing It in English: Asking for Clarification 35
Grammar Review: *I Have* 36
Grammar Review: Asking Questions with *Where* 37
More Reading and Writing: More about Peter Baraban 38
Doing It in English: Keeping in Touch (Greetings) 40
Doing It in English: Keeping in Touch (Addressing Letters) 41
Doing It in English: Keeping in Touch (Telephone Numbers) 42
Test Yourself 43
Language Learning Diary 44

Unit 4   Working Hard in the Southwest   45

    More Reading and Writing: More about Ramon Ramirez   46
    Doing It in English: Telling Time   48
    Grammar Review: Simple Present Time   49
    Grammar Review: Simple Present Time   50
    Grammar Review: Asking Questions with *When*   51
    Vocabulary Review: Days of the Week   52
    Grammar Review: Using *At* and *On* (with Time Phrases)   53
    Doing It in English: Understanding Work Schedules   54
    Doing It in English: Reading Signs and Telling about Time   55
    Vocabulary Review: Work Verbs   56
    Test Yourself   57
    Language Learning Diary   58

Unit 5   Familiar Faces and Places in Miami   59

    More Reading and Writing: More about Avelino Gonzalez   60
    What about Your Neighborhood?   61
    Vocabulary Review: Foods   62
    Doing It in English: Making a Shopping List   63
    Doing It in English: Recognizing and Saying Prices   64
    Doing It in English: Scanning Supermarket Ads   66
    Vocabulary Review: Neighborhood Places   67
    Grammar Review: Present Continuous   68
    Grammar Review: Using Present Continuous for Short Answers   69
    Grammar Review: Connecting Two Sentences with *And* or *But*   70
    Test Yourself   71
    Language Learning Diary   72

Unit 6   Celebrating Together in Cerritos, California   73

    Grammar Review: Past Forms   74
    Grammar Review: The Future with *Be Going To*   76
    Grammar Review: *In* and *On* with Dates   77
    Vocabulary Review: Months of the Year   78
    Doing It in English: Writing Dates   79
    Doing It in English: Describing the Weather   80
    Doing It in English: Reading a Calendar   81
    More Reading and Writing: More about the Chinese Wedding   82
    Test Yourself   84
    Language Learning Diary   85

Answer Key   87

Unit 1
Learning about Each Other in San Diego

When to Do Your Workbook Pages

Page		Do after Student Book Page	Page		Do after Student Book Page
2	**Grammar Review** The Verb *Be*	3	7	**Doing It in English** Filling Out a Form	11
3	**Doing It in English** Recognizing the Numbers 1 to 100	3	8	**Grammar Review** *There Is* and *There Are*	13
4	**Doing It in English** Writing Numbers 1 to 100	3	9	**Grammar Review** Noun Plurals	13
5	**Grammar Review** Making Sentences with *Be*	11	10–11	**Vocabulary Review** Things You Like to Do	14
6	**Doing It in English** Asking and Answering Personal Questions	11	12–14	**More Reading and Writing** More About Phuong Viet Duo	15
			15	**Test Yourself**	17
			16	**Language Learning Diary**	17

Be	
I **am**	from Mexico.
You **are**	from the U.S.
She **is**	from Korea.
He **is**	from Italy.
We **are**	from Poland.
They **are**	from El Salvador.

Fill in the blanks with the correct form of *be*.

A.

I ___am___ Lazar Dimitrijev. I _____
  1   2

28 years old. My wife and I _____
                                        3

from the former Yugoslav Republic of

Macedonia. We have two children.

Biljana _____ five years old and Ivo
            4

_____ four. We miss our country,
  5

but we _____ happy here.
            6

B.

My name ___is___ Sen Pao
                1

Chen. I _____ from China.
              2

I have two sons. They

_____ here with me.
  3

My birthdate _____ May 5,
                          4

1928. I _____ old, but I
            5

feel young!

Circle the correct number.
Try not to look at the box in the corner!

1.	thirty	20	13	(30)	50
2.	fifty-six	56	16	15	65
3.	fourteen	44	14	40	4
4.	ninety-seven	79	77	97	77
5.	seventy	70	17	7	77
6.	twenty-eight	38	18	28	82
7.	eighteen	8	88	80	18
8.	eleven	7	11	12	100
9.	forty-four	44	14	40	4
10.	sixty-five	56	15	65	64
11.	seventy-two	72	62	27	17
12.	eighty-nine	98	19	89	18
13.	fifteen	15	50	55	5
14.	thirty-nine	29	38	39	93
15.	thirteen	33	30	3	13

Numbers	
1	one
2	two
3	three
4	four
5	five
6	six
7	seven
8	eight
9	nine
10	ten
11	eleven
12	twelve
13	thirteen
14	fourteen
15	fifteen
16	sixteen
17	seventeen
18	eighteen
19	nineteen
20	twenty
21	twenty-one
22	twenty-two
30	thirty
40	forty
50	fifty
60	sixty
70	seventy
80	eighty
90	ninety
100	one hundred

Practice writing these numbers.

1.	20	_____ twenty _____
2.	4	_____ four _____
3.	50	_____
4.	15	_____
5.	2	_____
6.	70	_____
7.	11	_____
8.	30	_____
9.	5	_____
10.	10	_____
11.	100	_____
12.	9	_____
13.	40	_____
14.	6	_____
15.	80	_____

Grammar Review: Making Sentences with *Be*

Make a chart. Give information about family members or important people in your life.

Important People in my Life

Name	Age	Country	Marital Status

Now write about some of these people.

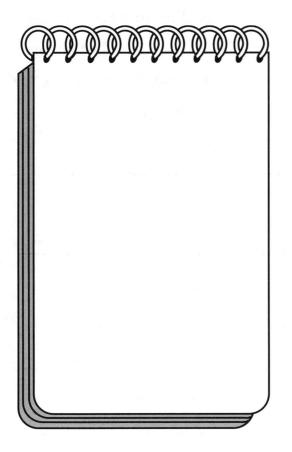

This is what Lazar Dimitrijev wrote:

Stela is my wife. She is twenty-five years old. She is married! My children are Ivo and Biljana. Ivo is four years old. Biljana is five.

·······Doing It
in English: Asking and Answering Personal Questions

A. Find out about this woman. Match the questions and answers.

1. What is your name?	**a.** Yes, I have two.
2. Please spell that.	**b.** I'm from Russia.
3. Where are you from?	**c.** It's Rina Martemianova.
4. Are you married?	**d.** M-A-R-T-E-M-I-A-N-O-V-A.
5. Do you have children?	**e.** It's May 5, 1943.
6. What is your birthdate?	**f.** Yes, I am.

B. What about you?

What is your name? _____

Please spell that. _____

Where are you from? _____

Are you married? _____

Do you have children? _____

What is your birthdate? _____

Doing It in English: Filling Out a Form

Fill out the large form with your information.
Please print clearly.

Name:	Avetov	Arkady
	(Last)	(First)

Address: 313 Los Feliz St
(Number and Street)
San Diego
(City)

CA	92037
(State)	(Zip Code)
619	324-8900
(Area Code)	(Phone Number)

Native Country: Russia

Birthdate: January 29, 1927

Signature: *Avetov Arkady*   Date: February 7, 1994

Name: _____ _____
       (Last)   (First)

Address: _____
                  (Number and Street)

_____
            (City)

_____   _____
 (State)   (Zip Code)

_____   _____
(Area Code)   (Phone Number)

Native Country: _____

Birthdate: _____

Signature: _____ Date: _____

Months

1	2	3
January	February	March
4	5	6
April	May	June
7	8	9
July	August	September
10	11	12
October	November	December

·······Grammar Review: *There Is* and *There Are*

> **There is** one student from Cambodia.
> **There are** two students from China.

A. Fill in the blanks with *there is* or *there are*.

In Eileen Schmitz's class, ____*there are*____ students from all over the world.

_____ one woman from Vietnam.

_____ five people from Russia.

_____ one person from Eritrea.

_____ two men from China.

B. What about your class? Fill in the blanks with numbers.

In my class, there are _____ students.

There are _____ men and

_____ women.

Grammar Review: Noun Plurals

Noun Plurals		
-s	**-es**	**-ies**
book books	class class**es**	country countr**ies**
pencil pencil**s**	bus bus**es**	city cit**ies**
boy boy**s**	church church**es**	story stor**ies**
Irregular Plurals		
	child child**ren**	
	person pe**ople**	
	woman wom**en**	
	man m**en**	

p 516

p 516

Read about this class from Chicago. Make the nouns plural.

There are ten _____students_____ in our class. There are two _____
(student) 1   (man) 2

and eight _____ . Two _____ are from Mexico and seven
(woman) 3   (person) 4

_____ are from Puerto Rico. The teacher is from the U.S. In class, we
(person) 5

read many _____ . We also write _____ about our
(book) 6   (story) 7

_____ . We talk about our _____ . Sometimes we talk
(family) 8   (country) 9

about our _____. I hope my future _____ are just like this!
(problem) 10   (class) 11

A. Fill out the questionnaire. Check **YES** or **NO**.

? ? ? ? ? ? ? Questionnaire ? ? ? ? ? ?

	YES	NO
Do you like to		
—play soccer?	❏	❏
—read?	❏	❏
—watch TV?	❏	❏
—cook?	❏	❏
—shop?	❏	❏
—fish?	❏	❏
—dance?	❏	❏
—sleep?	❏	❏
—listen to the radio?	❏	❏
—play an instrument?	❏	❏
—ride a bike?	❏	❏
—swim?	❏	❏
—roller skate?	❏	❏

B. Write what you like to do on the weekend.

My Weekend Activities

On Saturday mornings, I like to _____ or

_____. In the afternoon or evening, I like

to _____.

On Sundays, I often like to _____.

Sometimes I like to _____ or

_____.

······ More Reading and Writing: More about Phuong Viet Duo

A. Read more of Phuong Viet's story.

I am from Vietnam. It's a small country in Asia. It is beautiful. There are many lakes and rivers and rice. I miss it. I am homesick. Please help my country because it is poor. Thank you!

I have a big family in Vietnam. They live in a small town. The weather there is hot and wet. Many people work in the rice fields.

Phuong Viet Duo studies English in the Fairfax County Adult Education Program in Virginia.

B. Now fill in the blanks in Phuong Viet's story.

I _____am_____ from Vietnam. It's a small country

_____ Asia. It is beautiful. There are many lakes and

rivers _____ rice. I miss it. I _____

homesick. Please help my country because it _____

poor. Thank you!

I have a _____ family in Vietnam. They live in a

_____ town. The weather there _____

hot and wet. Many _____ work in the rice fields.

Look back at the story and check your answers.

C. What about you? Write about your country. Use the words in the boxes if you wish.

I am from _____ . It is a

_____ country in _____ .

big
small

Africa
Asia
Australia
Europe
North America
South America

There are many _____ and _____ .

lakes
rivers
trees
mountains
beaches

lakes
rivers
trees
mountains
beaches

The weather there is _____ .

hot
cold
wet
dry
beautiful

1. Lazar Dimitrijev and his wife _____*are*_____ from the former Yugoslav Republic of Macedonia.

a) are   b) is   c) am

2. They like to read and _____ to the radio.

a) play   b) watch   c) listen

3. There are eighteen _____ in Eileen Schmitz's class.

a) student   b) people   c) person

4. _____ are you from?

a) Where   b) What   c) Do

5. "Are you _____ ?"

"No, I'm single."

a) from Russia   b) thirty-five years old   c) married

6. Our teacher _____ married.

a) are   b) is   c) am

7. There _____ two students from China in the class.

a) are   b) is   c) am

8. Sen Pao Chen has two _____ .

a) children   b) child   c) people

······ Language Learning Diary

This week I learned

This week I spoke English to

This week I read

My new words are

I want to learn

Unit 2

Helping Each Other Learn in Chicago

When to Do Your Workbook Pages

Page		Do after Student Book Page	Page		Do after Student Book Page
18	**Grammar Review** *Like* + Infinitive	22	22	**Doing It in English** Reading School Signs	27
19	**Grammar Review** *Always, Often, Sometimes,* and *Never*	23	23	**Doing It in English** Finding Your Way Around School	27
20	**Vocabulary Review** Classroom Verbs	23	24–25	**More Reading and Writing** More About Adam Czerw	28
21	**Vocabulary Review** Classroom Objects	27	26–28	**Doing It in English** Asking Questions in Class	30
			29	**Test Yourself**	34
			30	**Language Learning Diary**	34

Grammar Review: *Like* + Infinitive

What do you like to do at school?

Write five sentences.

speak English
speak my language
speak to friends
work alone
work with a partner
work with a group
read stories
listen to the teacher
come late to class
write at the board
write at my desk

Things I Really Like to Do at School

1. I like to

2.

3.

4.

5.

I like to work with a partner.

Dominika Szmerdt is from Poland, and she studies at the University of Colorado in Boulder.

Grammar
Review: *Always, Often, Sometimes,* and *Never*

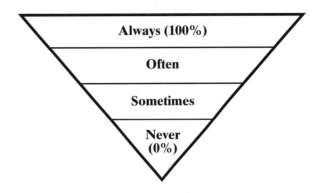

How do you learn? Fill in the blanks with *always, often, sometimes,* or *never.*

1. I _____ speak in class.

2. I _____ write new words in my notebook.

3. I _____ listen to the students in my class.

4. I _____ watch TV in English.

5. I _____ speak English outside of class.

6. I _____ study English with a friend.

7. I _____ listen to music in English.

8. I _____ ask questions when I don't understand.

Vocabulary Review: Classroom Verbs

Write a word or words next to each picture. The words in the box will help you.

1.  write at the board

2.  _____

3.  _____

4.  _____

5. _____ _____

6.  _____

7.  _____

8.  _____

9.  _____

10.  _____

work with a partner	laugh
✔ write at the board	ask a question
work with a group	speak
write at a desk	listen
stay in one's seat	read stories

Vocabulary Review: Classroom Objects

Label things in this classroom.
The words in the box will help you.

chalk

books

✔ books	teacher
✔ chalk	screen
blackboard	map
pictures	notebook
chairs	overhead projector (OHP)

······ Doing It in English: Reading School Signs

Which signs do you understand? Put a check (✔) by those signs.

Which signs are in your school?

Doing It in English: Finding Your Way Around School

A. Does your school have these? Write the words under the pictures.

rest rooms
pay phones
vending machine
stairs
library
cafeteria

restrooms
_____
1

_____
2

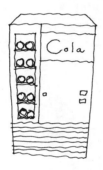

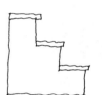

_____
3

_____
4

_____
5

_____
6

B. Now practice asking directions to:

the library

the stairs

the cafeteria

the pay phones

the vending machines

the rest rooms

Excuse me, where is the library?

Excuse me, where are the stairs?

When I came to the United States, I was alone. But in my English class, we work together. I have a lot of friends. It really changed my life.

The best thing about the class is the friendly atmosphere. I learn more because I really like the class. I meet many interesting people, and we talk in English.

Adam Czerw is from Poland. He studies English in Chicago with his friends. Adam is the third person from the right in the photo.

A. Write four words or phrases that you want to learn.

_____   _____

_____   _____

B. How are you like Adam? Circle **YES** or **NO**.

When I came to the United States, I was alone.	**YES**	**NO**
In my English class, we work together.	**YES**	**NO**
I have a lot of friends in class.	**YES**	**NO**
I have a friendly class.	**YES**	**NO**
I meet many interesting people.	**YES**	**NO**
We talk in English.	**YES**	**NO**

C. Copy your **YES** sentences here.

_____

_____

_____

_____

_____

_____

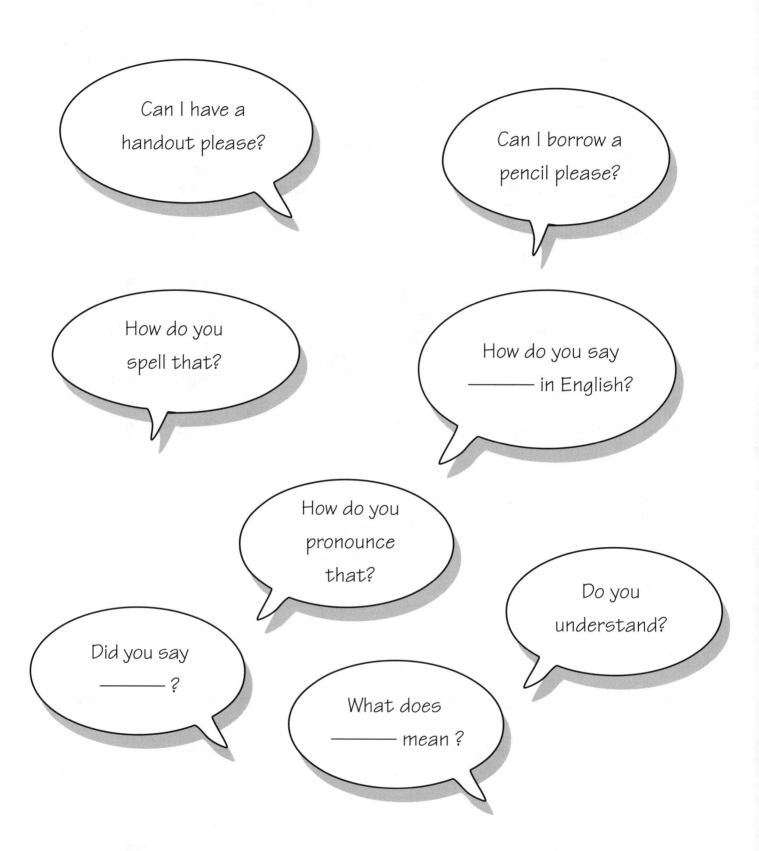

A. Practice saying the questions.

B. Ask questions in class. Record your questions here.

Date	My Question	I Asked (Who?)

C. Listen to your classmates' questions. Record some.

My Classmates' Questions

1. _____ ?

2. _____ ?

3. _____ ?

4. _____ ?

5. _____ ?

6. _____ ?

7. _____ ?

8. _____ ?

9. _____ ?

10. _____ ?

Test Yourself

1. I like to _____read_____ stories.

   a) reading   (b) read   c) reads

2. There are pictures and _____ in our classroom.

   a) maps   b) listen   c) write

3. Juan _____ speaks English in class.

   a) alone   b) often   c) listens

4. Excuse me, where _____ the library?

   a) it   b) are   c) is

5. How do you _____ your name?

   a) spell   b) have   c) mean

6. I like to work _____ a partner.

   a) at   b) my   c) with

7. Where are the _____ rooms?

   a) rest   b) offices   c) machines

8. The sign says, "No food or _____ ."

   a) men   b) women   c) drink

······ Language Learning Diary

This week I learned
This week I spoke English to
This week I read
My new words are
I want to learn

Unit 3

No Place Like Home: Stories from Massachusetts

When to Do Your Workbook Pages

Page		Do after Student Book Page	Page		Do after Student Book Page
32	**Vocabulary Review** Verbs	36	38-39	**More Reading and Writing** More about Peter Baraban	43
33	**Vocabulary Review** Family Words	38	40	**Doing It in English** Keeping in Touch (Greetings)	47
34	**Grammar Review** Using *In* and *On* with Place Names	39	41	**Doing It in English** Keeping in Touch (Addressing Letters)	47
35	**Doing It in English** Asking for Clarification	39	42	**Doing It in English** Keeping in Touch (Telephone Numbers)	47
36	**Grammar Review** *I have*	42	43	**Test Yourself**	48
37	**Grammar Review** Asking Questions with *Where*	42	44	**Language Learning Diary**	48

Vocabulary Review: Verbs

Do you remember Narin Sao's story? Now you can write a story too.

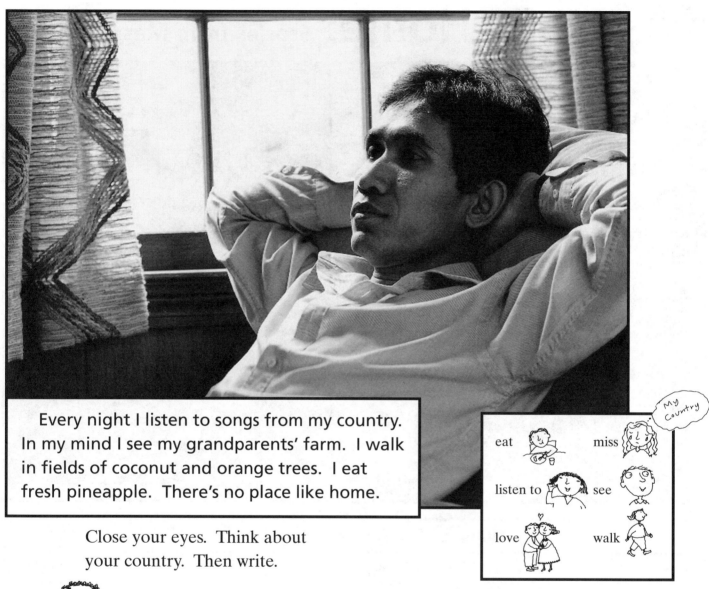

Every night I listen to songs from my country. In my mind I see my grandparents' farm. I walk in fields of coconut and orange trees. I eat fresh pineapple. There's no place like home.

My Country

eat   miss

listen to   see

love   walk

Close your eyes. Think about your country. Then write.

I see _____.

I walk _____.

I eat _____.

I listen to _____.

I love _____.

I miss _____.

Vocabulary Review: Family Words

A. Fill in the blanks.

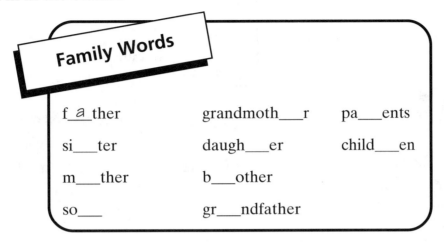

Family Words

f _a_ ther	grandmoth___r	pa___ents
si___ter	daugh___er	child___en
m___ther	b___other	
so___	gr___ndfather	

B. This is Carmen's family. Who are the people? Tell your ideas.

This is Carmen.

This picture is by Carmen Lomas Garza.
She is a Mexican painter.

······ Grammar
Review: Using *In* and *On* with Place Names

Fill in the blanks with *in* or *on*.

city		avenue
in + state	**on** +	street
country		road

A. I live ___in___ Phoenix, Arizona. My
1

apartment is ___on___ Alameda Avenue. My
2

family lives nearby, _____ Fourth Street.
3

Veronika Argueda is from Nicaragua.

B. I live _____ the United States, _____ New
1   2

Jersey. My family still lives _____ Seoul.
3

It is _____ Korea.
4

Paul Lee

C. Now I live _____ the United States. I came
1

in 1991. My family lives _____ Chihuahua, a
2

big city _____ Mexico. I live _____ Santa
3   4

Fe, _____ Agua Fria Street. I want my
5

family to come.

Nancy Rascon

Write conversations with these sentences. Then practice the conversations.

1. On Maple St.
   Excuse me?
   Where do you live?
   Oh, yes.
   Maple St.

2. OK, thanks.
   Aziz.
   What is your last name?
   Please spell it.
   A-Z-I-Z.

3. Peter Lee.
   Excuse me?
   What is your name?
   Peter. Peter Lee.
   Nice to meet you Peter.

4. Where does your son live?
   Your son. Where does he live?
   I don't understand.
   Oh! In Haiti!

Grammar Review: *I Have*

Check **YES** or **NO**.

	YES	NO
I have a wife.	❏	❏
I have a husband.	❏	❏
I have one sister.	❏	❏
I have two sisters.	❏	❏
I have _____ sisters.	❏	❏
I have one brother.	❏	❏
I have two brothers.	❏	❏
I have _____ brothers.	❏	❏
I have one son.	❏	❏
I have two sons.	❏	❏
I have _____ sons.	❏	❏
I have one daughter.	❏	❏
I have two daughters.	❏	❏
I have _____ daughters.	❏	❏
I have _____.	❏	❏
I have _____.	❏	❏

I have one son, a husband, two sisters, and a mother.

Write a sentence with your **YES** information.

_____

_____

_____

_____

Tamara Berman is from Russia. She studies English at the University of New Mexico.

Grammar Review: Asking Questions with *Where*

Where **do** you **live?**	I **live** in Los Angeles.
Where **does** your sister **live?**	She **lives** in Puerto Rico.
Where **does** your brother **live?**	He **lives** here, with me.
Where **do** your parents **live?**	They **live** in Somalia.

Write questions. Then practice saying them.

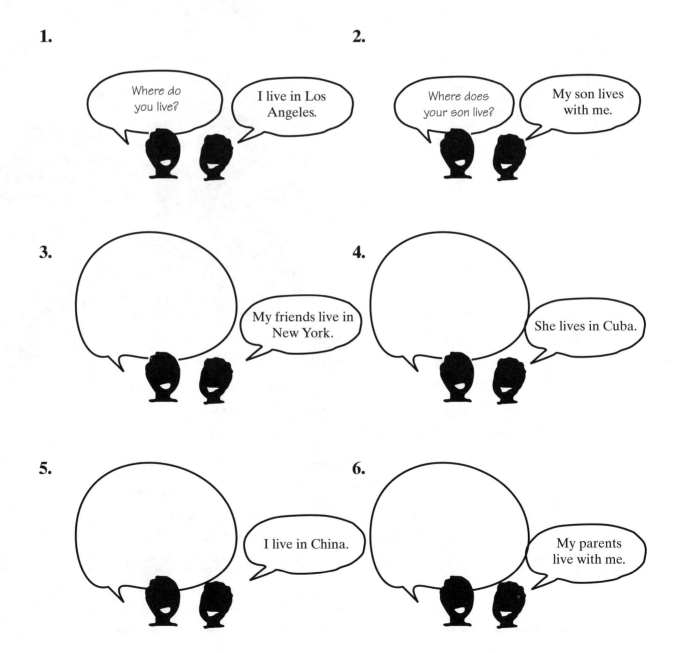

1.

Where do you live?

I live in Los Angeles.

2.

Where does your son live?

My son lives with me.

3.

My friends live in New York.

4.

She lives in Cuba.

5.

I live in China.

6.

My parents live with me.

More Reading
and Writing: More about Peter Baraban

A. Read more of Peter's story.
How is he like you?
How is he different from you?

I have lived in America for one year and four months. I grew up in the former Soviet Union. I'm always thinking about my country because it is my homeland. Almost all my family—my parents, brothers, and sisters—are there. I want them to come here.

I live with my wife. We bought a house with a good garden. We have children. We have one son and two daughters. I am happy with them. I was happy when my son started to walk. I was happy when he said his first word, "Papa." I am happy that we live in America.

Peter Baraban lives in Greenfield, Massachusetts. He studies English at Greenfield Community College.

B. How is Peter like you? How is he different? Fill out the diagram below.

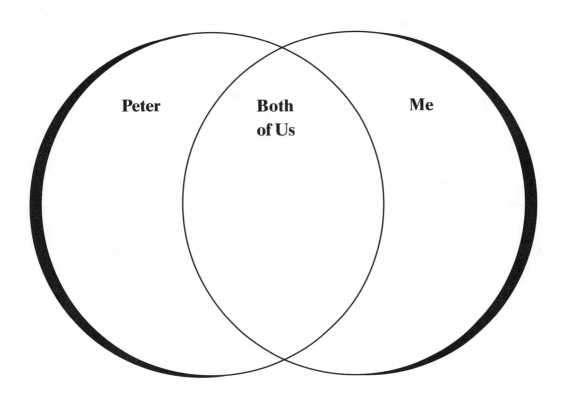

Peter

Both of Us

Me

This is what Rika Asakura wrote.

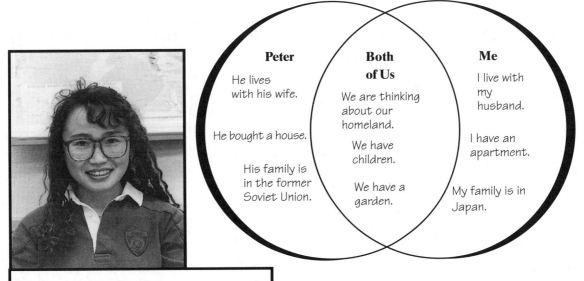

Peter

He lives with his wife.

He bought a house.

His family is in the former Soviet Union.

Both of Us

We are thinking about our homeland.

We have children.

We have a garden.

Me

I live with my husband.

I have an apartment.

My family is in Japan.

Rika Asakura is Japanese. She studies at the University of New Mexico.

Casual Greetings (for family, friends, and classmates)	**More Formal Greetings** (for strangers and acquaintances)
_____ *Hi!*	_____ *Hello.*
_____ *How's it going?*	_____ *Good morning.*
_____ *Howdy!*	_____ *Good afternoon.*
_____ *What's up?*	_____ *Good evening.*

A. Which greetings do you know? Put a check (✔) next to the greetings you know.

B. What do you say to

1. your classmates? _____

2. your neighbors? _____

3. your teacher? _____

C. Listen to people at school or at another public place. How do they greet each other? Write what you hear.

_____

_____

_____

_____

_____

_____

Doing It in English: Keeping in Touch (Addressing Letters)

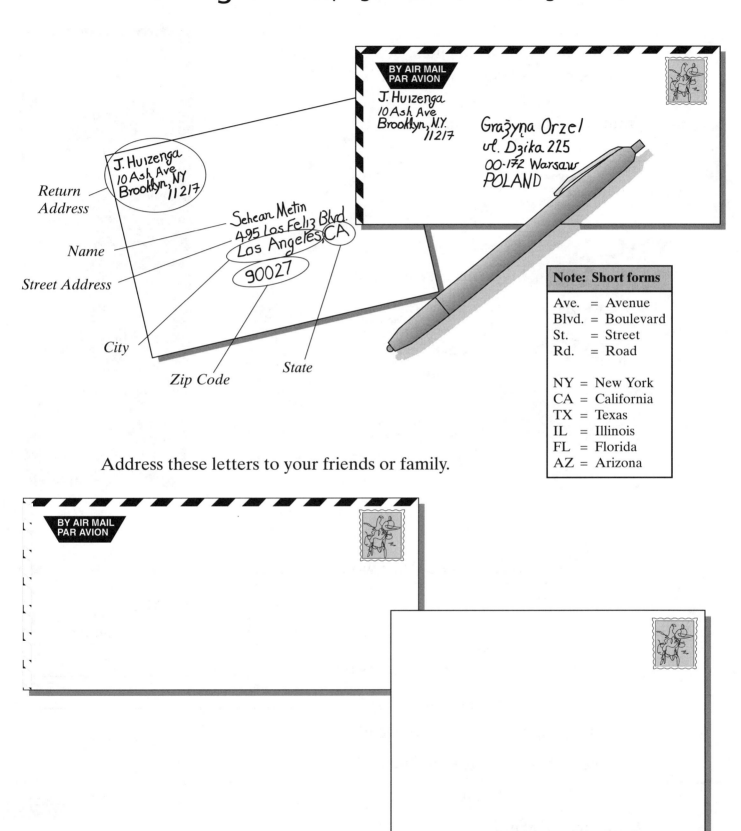

Address these letters to your friends or family.

Note: Short forms

Ave.	= Avenue
Blvd.	= Boulevard
St.	= Street
Rd.	= Road

NY	= New York
CA	= California
TX	= Texas
IL	= Illinois
FL	= Florida
AZ	= Arizona

Doing It in English: Keeping in Touch (Telephone Numbers)

This is a page from a telephone book.
Vince Sanchez's telephone number is
471-2439
(four seven one—two four three nine).

SANCHEZ V – SCARBOROUGH

SANCHEZ Vince	
1003 Caile De Suenos	471-2439
Waldo 528 Airport Rd.	471-0132
Willie J M 802 Don Cubero Av	982-9326
Yvette 338 Don Cubero Pl	982-3139
SANCHEZ-MARTINEZ T	
Camp Stoney Rd.	988-3259
SANDELIN Jay Rancho Elisa	984-8608
Jay E Rt 7 Hyde Park Rd.	982-0246
Kent 1027 Canyon Rd.	989-7094
SANDER J 2800 Cerrilos Rd.	438-8514
SANDERFORD William	
31 Herrada Rd.	989-4111
SANDERS A L R Camino Pinones	983-3231
Alison Tann Rd.	983-6235

Read the telephone number. Then write the number and the name.

		NUMBER	NAME
1.	nine eight three—three two three one	983-3231	ALR Sanders
2.	four seven one—zero one three two	_____	_____
3.	nine eight four—eight six zero eight	_____	_____
4.	nine eight eight—three two five nine	_____	_____
5.	nine eight two—three one three nine	_____	_____
6.	four three eight—eight five one four	_____	_____

My phone number is _____.

Test Yourself

1. Jorge lives _____ Fifth Avenue.

   a) at   b) on   c) in

2. Narin Sao _____ songs from his country.

   a) listens to   b) sees   c) eats

3. Where _____ you live?

   a) do   b) does   c) are

4. Kim has two _____—a son and a daughter.

   a) sisters   b) parents   c) children

5. My family lives _____ Japan.

   a) at   b) on   c) in

6. Write a _____ on your letter.

   a) zip code   b) telephone   c) visit

7. I _____ two sisters and a brother.

   a) home   b) live   c) have

8. My _____ live with me.

   a) son   b) parents   c) sister

Language Learning Diary

This week I learned
This week I spoke English to
This week I read
My new words are
I want to learn

When to Do Your Workbook Pages

Page		Do after Student Book Page	Page		Do after Student Book Page
46–47	**More Reading and Writing** More about Ramon Ramirez	51	53	**Grammar Review** Using *At* and *On* (with Time Phrases)	57
48	**Doing It in English** Telling Time	52	54	**Doing It in English** Understand Work Schedules	57
49	**Grammar Review** Simple Present	52	55	**Doing It in English** Reading Signs and Telling About Time	57
50	**Grammar Review** Simple Present	53	56	**Vocabulary Review** Work Verbs	61
51	**Grammar Review** Asking Questions with *When*	56	57	**Test Yourself**	63
52	**Vocabulary Review** Days of the Week	57	58	**Language Learning Diary**	63

More Reading
and Writing: More about Ramon Ramirez

A. Read more of Ramon's story.

My Busy Day

I start work at 5:00 in the morning. For breakfast, I cook steak, eggs, bacon, and pancakes. I work from 5:00 A.M. to 1:30 P.M. Sometimes I work from 5:00 A.M. to 5:00 P.M. I'm a morning person. I have to be!

Sometimes I get a break for lunch. But sometimes I work ten hours without a break. From 5:00 A.M. to 3:00 P.M. without a break! That's a big problem here. There aren't enough chefs. Sometimes I'm the only chef. There are forty people in the restaurant, and I'm cooking for all of them. That's too many people. Sometimes I get mad and want to quit.

Ramon Ramirez studies and works
in Santa Fe, New Mexico.

B. What do you think?

	I Agree (YES)	I Disagree (NO)
1. Ramon has a good job.	❏	❏
2. Ramon works hard.	❏	❏
3. Ramon likes his job.	❏	❏
4. Ramon has a good boss.	❏	❏

C. Write about *your* busy day.

My Busy Day

I get up at _____. For breakfast,

I eat _____.

I start to work* at _____.

I usually work from _____ to

_____. Sometimes I work _____

hours a day. I go to bed at _____.

*Work also can be schoolwork or housework!

Doing It in English: Telling Time

Read the time. Then match it to a clock.

1. It's ten o'clock.   **a.**

2. It's four thirty.   **b.**

3. It's seven forty-five.   **c.**

4. It's seven fifteen.   **d.**

5. It's three o'clock.   **e.**

6. It's two thirty-five.   **f.**

7. It's one fifty-five.   **g.**

8. It's nine thirty.   **h.**

9. It's ten twenty-five.   **i.**

10. It's four fifty.   **j.**

Grammar Review: Simple Present

Write your typical daily activities. For example, you can write, *I get up, I go to work, I eat lunch,* and so on.

Time   **My Day**

Time	
A.M. 6:00	
6:30	
7:00	
7:30	
8:00	
8:30	
9:00	
9:30	
10:00	
10:30	
11:00	
11:30	
12:00	
P.M. 12:30	
1:00	
1:30	
2:00	
2:30	
3:00	
3:30	
4:00	
4:30	
5:00	
5:30	
6:00	
6:30	
7:00	
7:30	
8:00	
8:30	
9:00	
9:30	
10:00	
10:30	
11:00	
11:30	
12:00	

Grammar Review: Simple Present

Fill in the blanks with the correct form of the verb.

Dolores Porras Enriques is an artist. She

_____works_____ hard. She _____
(work) 1   (make) 2

Mexican plates and pots from clay. Her husband

_____ her. When she _____
(help) 3   (finish) 4

a plate, her husband _____ it with
                          (paint) 5

beautiful colors.

Dolores Enriques and her husband are from Mexico.
In the summer, they work in New Mexico.

Simple Present	
I You We They } **work** hard.	She He } **works** hard.

Grammar Review: Asking Questions with *When*

Simple Present	
When **do** you **eat** breakfast?	I **eat** breakfast at 7:30.
When **do** you **go** to work?	I **go** to work at about 8:00 A.M.

Write questions. Then practice saying them.

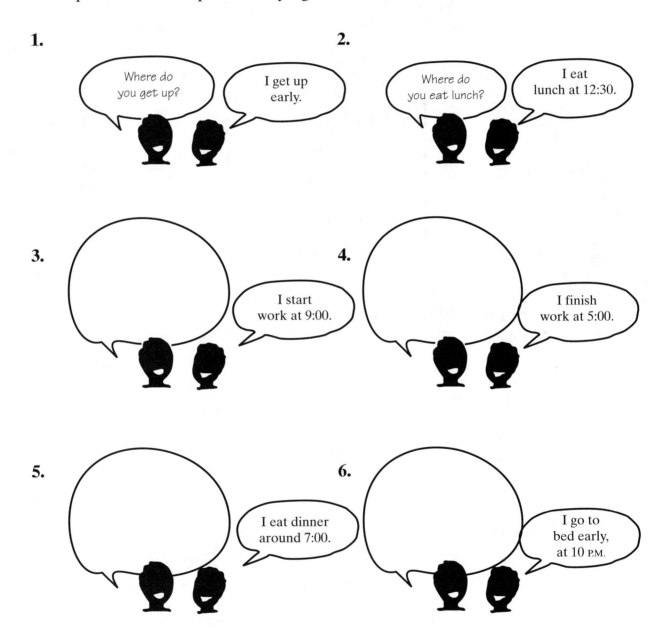

1.
Where do you get up?

I get up early.

2.
Where do you eat lunch?

I eat lunch at 12:30.

3.
I start work at 9:00.

4.
I finish work at 5:00.

5.
I eat dinner around 7:00.

6.
I go to bed early, at 10 P.M.

Vocabulary Review: Days of the Week

A. Fill in the blanks.

Days of the Week

Mond_a_ y

Tue___day

Wedne___day

Th___rsday

Fr___day

Sa___urday

Su___day

Short Forms

Mon.
Tues.
Wed.
Thurs.
Fri.
Sat.
Sun.

B. Complete the sentences.

1. Today is _____.

2. My favorite day is _____.

3. I shop on _____.

4. I relax on _____.

5. I get up early on _____.

6. I go to school on _____.

Grammar
Review: Using *At* and *On* (with Time Phrases)

A. Do you remember Khampoo's story? Read it again.
Circle *at* and *on*.

Note:	
at	5:15
at	8:00
on	Friday
on	Monday

I leave my first job (at) 2:00 P.M. I pick up my son from school. When my wife gets home at 4:00, I go to my second job. Sometimes I work overtime on Saturday. On Sunday we go to the supermarket.

B. What about you? Tell when. Use *at* or *on*.

1. I go to work _____.

2. I go to school _____.

3. I go to the supermarket _____.

4. I get up _____.

5. I go to bed _____.

Doing It in English: Understanding Work Schedules

Work Schedule			
	Ramona	**Lee**	**Inez**
Mon.	9-6	8-5	
Tues.	9-6	8-5	
Wed.		9-6	8-5
Thurs.	12-8		8-5
Fri.	12-8		9-6
Sat.	10-4	10-4	
Sun.		10-4	10-4

Days	Short Form
Monday	Mon.
Tuesday	Tues.
Wednesday	Wed.
Thursday	Thurs.
Friday	Fri.
Saturday	Sat.
Sunday	Sun.

© Ken Light

Look at the work schedule. Answer these questions.

1. When does Inez work on Wednesday?   _from 8:00 to 5:00_
2. When does Ramona work on Friday?   _____
3. When does Lee work on Saturday?   _____
4. When does Inez work on Friday?   _____
5. Who works on Saturday?   _____
6. Who works on Sunday?   _____

Answer the questions by *speaking*.

1. When is it open on Sunday?
2. When is it open on Saturday?

noon = 12:00 P.M.

3. When is it open on Friday?
4. When is it open on Saturday?
5. When is it open on Sunday?
6. When is it open on Wednesday?

Vocabulary Review: Work Verbs

A. Match the words and pictures.

1. sew

2. grow vegetables

3. knit

4. paint a picture

5. fix a car

6. take care of children

7. cook

8. clean

9. paint walls

10. fix a sink

a.

b.

c.

d.

e.

f.

g.

h.

i.

j.

B. Write about yourself.

1. I can _____ very well.

2. I can _____ quite well.

3. But I cannot _____ !

1. Ramon can _____ eggs.

   a) sew   b) clean   c) cook

2. Khampoo goes to the supermarket _____ Sunday.

   a) on   b) at   c) in

3. Maria Fernandez _____ hard.

   a) work   b) works   c) working

4. I get _____ at 7:00 A.M.

   a) up   b) on   c) in

5. When _____ you start work?

   a) to   b) are   c) do

6. I go to bed _____ 11:00 P.M.

   a) at   b) on   c) in

7. Ramon usually works _____ 5:00 A.M. to 1:30 P.M.

   a) to   b) in   c) from

8. My mother _____ sew very well.

   a) to   b) can   c) works

Language Learning Diary

This week I learned
This week I spoke English to
This week I read
My new words are
I want to learn

Unit 5

Familiar Faces and Places in Miami

When to Do Your Workbook Pages

Page		Do after Student Book Page
60–61	**More Reading and Writing** More about Avelino Gonzalez	67
62	**Vocabulary Review** Foods	68
63	**Doing It in English** Making a Shopping List	68
64–65	**Doing It in English** Recognizing and Saying Prices	69
66	**Doing It in English** Scanning Supermarket Ads	70
67	**Vocabulary Review** Neighborhood Places	72

Page		Do after Student Book Page
68	**Grammar Review** Present Continuous	75
69	**Grammar Review** Present Continuous/ Short Answers	75
70	**Grammar Review** Connecting Two Sentences with *And* or *But*	76
71	**Test Yourself**	79
72	**Language Learning Diary**	79

More Reading and Writing: More about Avelino Gonzalez

Read more about Avelino.

In Little Havana, in Miami, I can find everything from my country—Cuban coffee, mangoes, papayas, and pineapples. I can find my people, too. It feels like home!

This neighborhood is very friendly. People help each other. The rent is low here. These are the good things.

But Little Havana is a little dangerous. There's a lot of crime. Some parts are dirty. There are some homeless people here too.

Avelino Gonzalez comes from Cuba and lives in Miami.

What about Your Neighborhood?
Read the sentences and check **YES** or **NO.**

	YES	NO
In my neighborhood, I can find everything from my country.	❑	❑
I can find my people.	❑	❑
My neighborhood feels like home.	❑	❑
My neighborhood is friendly.	❑	❑
People here help each other.	❑	❑
The rent is low here.	❑	❑
My neighborhood is a little dangerous.	❑	❑
There's a lot of crime.	❑	❑
Some parts are dirty.	❑	❑
Some people in my neighborhood are homeless.	❑	❑

Copy your **YES** sentences here.

My Neighborhood

_____

_____

_____

_____

_____

_____

_____

_____

_____

Vocabulary Review: Foods

A. Do you remember the names of these foods? Write them.

Foods

1. _____ eggs _____

2. _____

3. _____

4. _____

5. _____

6. _____

7. _____

8. _____

B. Put these foods and drinks into two groups.

pineapples	coffee	chicken
apples	steak	pizza
pears	eggs	fish
carrots	cake	rice
garlic	melon	mangoes
cola		

Things I Like	Things I Don't Like

Doing It in English: Making a Shopping List

This is Avelino's shopping list. Now make *your* shopping list. Write the foods and drinks you need to buy.

Use the words in the box or your dictionary to help you.

oranges
apples
rice
bread
milk
orange juice
coffee
tea

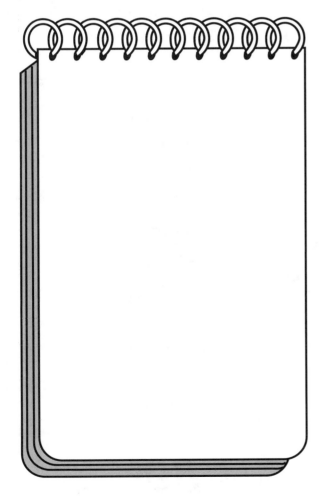

Fruits	**Meats**
apples	chicken
bananas	ground beef
oranges	lamb
grapes	steak
lemons	pork chops

Vegetables	**Sweets**
potatoes	sugar
lettuce	cookies
carrots	cake
peppers	candy
onions	chocolate
garlic	donuts

Drinks	**Other**
juice	bread
cola	rice
water	noodles
coffee	beans
tea	tortillas

Dairy Products

milk
cheese
eggs
yogurt

seventy-five cents

one dollar and fifty cents (one fifty)
a dollar fifty

ten dollars and twenty-five cents
ten twenty-five

twenty-one dollars and thirty cents
twenty-one thirty

A. Match the words and numbers. Practice saying them.

1. four ninety-nine			**a.**	**19¢**
2. one forty-nine			**b.**	**12⁹⁹**
3. eighty-nine cents			**c.**	**50¢**
4. twelve ninety-nine			**d.**	**4⁹⁹**
5. fifty cents			**e.**	**1⁷⁹**
6. a dollar seventy-nine			**f.**	**1⁴⁹**
7. nineteen cents			**g.**	**89¢**

B. Now practice saying and writing these prices.

1. **2⁹⁹** _____ two ninety-nine _____

2. **88¢** _____ eighty-eight cents _____

3. **69¢** _____

4. **$5** _____

5. **13⁴⁹** _____

6. **$10** _____

7. **3⁴⁹** _____

8. **6²⁷** _____

Numbers	
1	one
2	two
3	three
4	four
5	five
6	six
7	seven
8	eight
9	nine
10	ten
11	eleven
12	twelve
13	thirteen
14	fourteen
15	fifteen
16	sixteen
17	seventeen
18	eighteen
19	nineteen
20	twenty
21	twenty-one
22	twenty-two
30	thirty
40	forty
50	fifty
60	sixty
70	seventy
80	eighty
90	ninety
100	one hundred

Doing It in English: Scanning Supermarket Ads

Note: ea.   = each
        pkg. = package
        lb. = pound
        oz. = ounce

There are 16 ounces in a pound.

A. These ads were in the newspaper. Can you find the following information?

1. How much is a package of mushrooms?   _____69¢_____

2. How much are five bunches of radishes?   _____

3. How much are two heads of leaf lettuce? _____

4. How much is a bunch of celery?   _____

5. How much are two pounds of broccoli?   _____

B. Are these good prices? Which vegetables would you buy?

Vocabulary Review: Neighborhood Places

A. Check **YES** or **NO.**

In my neighborhood, there is a. . . .

	YES	NO
bank	❑	❑
shoe store	❑	❑
health clinic	❑	❑
laundromat	❑	❑
post office	❑	❑
police station	❑	❑
community center	❑	❑
supermarket	❑	❑
park	❑	❑

B. Fill in the blanks with one of the words above.

1. You can mail a letter at the _____*post office*_____.

2. You can buy food at the _____.

3. You can wash clothes at the _____.

4. You can get money at the _____.

5. You can buy shoes at the _____.

6. You can get medical help at the _____.

7. You can make new friends at the _____.

8. You can enjoy nature at the _____.

9. You can report a crime at the _____.

Grammar Review: Present Continuous

Write captions under these photos.
(A *caption* is a sentence under a picture
in a newspaper or book.) Follow the example.

Avelino is drinking Cuban coffee.

1. (Avelino . . . drink Cuban coffee)

2. (Avelino . . . shop at a supermarket)

_____

3. (Avelino and his friend . . . talk)

_____

4. (The men . . . play dominoes, and Avelino . . . watch them)

Grammar
        Review: Using Present Continuous/Short Answers

Answer these questions with short answers. Follow the examples.

1. Is he shopping for vegetables?

     No, he isn't.

2. Is he shopping for shoes?

     Yes, he is.

3. Are they talking?

     Yes, they are.

4. Are they playing dominoes?

5. Are they shopping?

6. Is he talking?

7. Is he drinking coffee?

8. Is he playing dominoes?

Review: Connecting Two Sentences with *And* or *But*

I came here in 1992, <u>and</u> my grandmother helped me a lot.   I lived in her house in Little Havana for a year, <u>but</u> she didn't take money for food or rent.

You can connect two sentences like this:
. . . . ., and . . . .
. . . . ., but . . . .

A. Fill in the blanks with *and* or *but*.

1. Avelino loves coffee, _____*and*_____ he drinks a lot of it.

2. His grandmother likes coffee, ____*but*____ she doesn't drink it often.

3. Aveli o eats Cuban food, _____ he doesn't make it often.

4. Avelino's grandmother likes Cuban food too, _____ she makes it often.

B. **What about you?** Fill in the blanks with the name of a food or drink. Then connect the sentences with *and* or *but*.

1. I love _____. I drink a lot of it.

_____

2. I like _____. I don't drink it often.

_____

3. I like to eat _____. I don't make it often.

_____

4. I like _____. I make it often.

_____

Test Yourself

1. You can wash clothes at the _____.

   a) park   b) laundromat   c) post office

2. Avelino loves to eat Cuban food, _____ he doesn't make it often.

   a) but   b) Avelino   c) and

3. Avelino _____ at the University of Miami.

   a) studying   b) study   c) is studying

4. The _____ is low in Little Havana, according to Avelino.

   a) crime   b) neighborhood   c) rent

5. Some people make a shopping _____ before they go to the supermarket.

   a) list   b) drink   c) chicken

6. A _____ of broccoli is 49¢.

   a) vegetable   b) pound   c) supermarket

7. "Are the men playing dominoes?"
   "Yes, they _____."

   a) is   b) are   c) aren't

8. You can mail a letter at the _____.

   a) police station   b) post office   c) bank

••••••• Language Learning Diary

This week I learned

This week I spoke English to

This week I read

My new words are

I want to learn

Unit 6 Celebrating Together in Cerritos, California

When to Do Your Workbook Pages

Page		Do after Student Book Page	Page		Do after Student Book Page
74–75	**Grammar Review** Past Forms	85	80	**Doing It in English** Describing the Weather	91
76	**Grammar Review** The Future with *Be Going To*	87	81	**Doing It in English** Reading a Calendar	91
77	**Grammar Review** *In* and *On* with Dates	90	82–83	**More Reading and Writing** More About the Chinese Wedding	93
78	**Vocabulary Review** Months of the Year	91	84	**Test Yourself**	96
79	**Doing It in English** Writing Dates	91	85	**Language Learning Diary**	96

Grammar Review: Past Forms

A. Write the past form of these verbs. Look in the box if you need help.

1. listen   _listened_
2. teach   _____
3. have   _____
4. give   _____
5. cook   _____
6. eat   _____
7. dance   _____
8. cry   _____
9. show   _____
10. look   _____
11. listen   _____
12. play   _____
13. decorate   _____
14. wear   _____

> had
> cooked
> looked
> taught
> played
> showed
> gave
> laughed
> ate
> wore
> cried
> danced
> listened
> decorated

B. Now put these verbs into two groups.

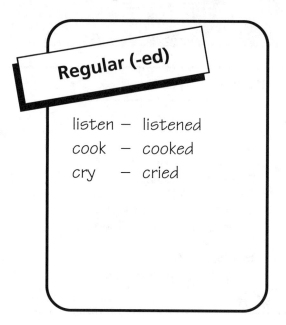

Regular (-ed)

listen — listened
cook — cooked
cry — cried

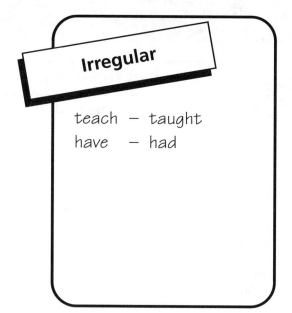

Irregular

teach — taught
have — had

C. Put the verbs in this story in the past.

We _____had_____ a wonderful Thanksgiving holiday. The whole family was
  1 (have)

together. I _____ a big turkey, potatoes, and pies. My husband and
  2 (cook)

mother _____ me a lot of help. Grandmother _____ me
  3 (give)   **4** (show)

how to make her special bread. My daughter _____ the table with our
  5 (decorate)

best dishes. We all _____ our best clothes. We _____ too
  6 (wear)   **7** (eat)

much and _____ until we _____. Everything was perfect!
  8 (laugh)   **9** (cry)

Linda Meyer lives with her family in Rochester, New York.

D. **What about you?** Think about a holiday you celebrated
recently.

1. What did you cook?   _____I cooked_____

2. What did you eat?   _____

3. What did you wear?   _____

4. What else did you do? _____

Grammar Review: The Future with *Be Going To*

Future with *Going To*
I **am** You **are** He or she **is**   } **going to make** a cake. We **are** They **are**
"Going to" sounds like "gonna" when people speak quickly.

My baby is going to have her first birthday. I am planning a big party. I am going to invite my family and friends and make a big cake. We're going to have a good time!

Eustolia Medina studies ESL at Santa Fe Community College in New Mexico. She is from Mexico.

Plan your next holiday or celebration.

Name of holiday or celebration _____

Date _____

I am going to cook _____.

I am going to eat _____.

I am going to go _____.

I am going to wear _____.

I am going to have a good time!

Grammar Review: *In* and *On* with Dates

These are some holidays in the U.S.

JANUARY	FEBRUARY	MARCH	APRIL
New Year's Day (January 1)	Valentine's Day (February 14)		
MAY	**JUNE**	**JULY**	**AUGUST**
Mother's Day	Father's Day	Independence Day (July 4)	
SEPTEMBER	**OCTOBER**	**NOVEMBER**	**DECEMBER**
	Halloween (October 31)	Thanksgiving	Christmas (December 25)

A. Fill in the blanks with *in* or *on*.

in October
on October 31

in January
on January 1

1. Mother's Day is _____in_____ May.

2. Christmas is _____on_____ December 25.

3. Halloween is _____ October 31.

4. Thanksgiving is _____ November.

5. New Year's Day is _____ January 1.

6. Father's Day is _____ June.

7. Independence Day is _____ July 4.

8. Valentine's Day is _____ February 14.

B. What about you?

1. My birthday is on _____.

2. My favorite holiday is in _____.

Vocabulary Review: Months of the Year

A. Fill in the missing letters in the calendar.

JANU __ __ Y	FEBRUA __ __	__ __ RCH	A __ __ IL
M __ __	JU __ __	J __ __ Y	AUGU __ __
__ __ PTEMBER	OCTOB __ __	N __ __ EMBER	DEC __ __ BER

B. Match the months with their abbreviations (short forms).

Mar.   February

Jan.   October

Dec.   March

Sept.   August

Feb.   September

Apr.   January

Nov.   November

Aug.   December

Oct.   April

> **NOTE:** There are no short forms for *May, June,* and *July.*

C. **What about you?** Write the name of a month.

1. My birthday is in _____.

2. My favorite holiday is in _____.

3. My favorite month is _____

because _____.

Doing It in English: Writing Dates

Date in Words	Date in Numbers
May 20, 1990	5/20/90
February 6, 1950	2/6/50

NOTE: In North America, write the month first.

A. Now write these dates in numbers.

1. October 4, 1995   _____10/4/95_____

2. January 25, 1980   _____1/25/80_____

3. August 2, 1994   _____

4. May 18, 1970   _____

5. July 4, 1996   _____

6. December 30, 1990   _____

7. March 1, 1995   _____

8. September 2, 1984   _____

B. What about you?

1. Your birthdate

_____ (in words)

_____ (in numbers)

2. Today's date

_____ (in words)

_____ (in numbers)

⬤⬤⬤⬤⬤⬤ Doing It in English: Describing the Weather

What are the seasons like in your country?
What are they like here?
Write about the weather in each season.

It's windy. It's sunny. It's rainy.

It's hot. It's snowy and cold. It's cloudy.

Seasons in my Country

Winter_____

Spring_____

Summer_____

Fall_____

Seasons Here

Winter_____

Spring_____

Summer_____

Fall_____

Winter	Spring	Summer	Fall
December January February	March April May	June July August	September October November

February

S	M	T	W	T	F	S
	1	2	3	4	5	6
7	8	9	10	11	12 Lincoln's Birthday	13
14 Valentine's Day	15	16	17	18	19	20
21	22 Washington's Birthday	23	24	25	26	27
28						

S   Sunday
M   Monday
T   Tuesday
W   Wednesday
T   Thursday
F   Friday
S   Saturday

NOTE: Sunday is the first day of the week on U.S. calendars.

Write the days of the week.

1. February 8 _____Monday_____

2. February 26 _____

3. Valentine's Day _____

4. February 17 _____

5. Lincoln's Birthday _____

6. February 2 _____

······ More Reading and Writing: More about the Chinese Wedding

A. Read more about the Chinese wedding. Circle new words. Can you guess their meaning?

For our celebration, we wanted more than just an exhibit. We wanted some activities. It's more fun! Weddings are very important for Chinese people. So we showed how to do a wedding. The man and woman bow to God, bow to the parents, and then to each other. Then they go to the love nest!

We picked the most beautiful bride for our wedding. We borrowed the wedding costumes from the Chinese Cultural Society. They are red. Red is a lucky color for the Chinese. Some people played music with Chinese instruments. The bride and groom had fun. We all did!

Jenny Chao is a student at ABC School, Cerritos, California. She is from China.

B. Cover the story on page 82. Now read the story again and write in the missing verbs.

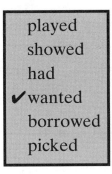

played
showed
had
✔wanted
borrowed
picked

For our celebration, we wanted more than just an exhibit. We

_____wanted_____ some activities. It's more fun! Weddings are

very important for Chinese people. So we _____

how to do a wedding. The man and woman bow to God, bow to the

parents, and then to each other. Then they go to the love nest!

We _____ the most beautiful bride for our wedding.

We _____ the wedding costumes from the Chinese

Cultural Society. They are red. Red is a lucky color for the Chinese.

Some people _____ music with Chinese instruments.

The bride and groom _____ fun. We all did!

1. Christmas is _____ December.

   a) on   b) in   c) at

2. Eustolia Medina is going _____ a big party for her baby.

   a) to have   b) have   c) having

3. Mother's Day is in _____.

   a) Christmas   b) May   c) Thanksgiving

4. The Chinese bride and groom _____ beautiful costumes.

   a) ate   b) wore   c) danced

5. Linda Meyer _____ a big turkey and potatoes for her Thanksgiving holiday.

   a) cooked   b) cook   c) cooking

6. The four seasons are winter, spring, summer, and _____.

   a) sunny   b) fall   c) windy

7. The summer months are June, July, and _____.

   a) May   b) September   c) August

8. 2/4/95 is _____.

   a) February 4, 1995   b) April 2, 1995   c) April 4, 1995

Language Learning Diary

This week I learned
This week I spoke English to
This week I read
My new words are
I want to learn

ANSWER KEY ● ● ●

Unit 1 ● ● ●

page 2:
A. 2. am   3. are   4. is
5. is   6. are

B. 2. am   3. are   4. is
5. am

page 3:
1. 30   2. 56   3. 14   4. 97
5. 70   6. 28   7. 18   8. 11
9. 44   10. 65   11. 72
12. 89   13. 15   14. 39
15. 13

page 4:
3. fifty   4. fifteen   5. two
6. seventy   7. eleven
8. thirty   9. five   10. ten
11. one hundred   12. nine
13. forty   14. six
15. eighty

page 5: Answers will vary.

page 6:
2. d   3. b   4. f   5. a
6. e

page 7: Answers will vary.

page 8:
A. *There is* one woman
from Vietnam.
There are five people
from Russia.
There is one person
from Eritrea.
There are two men
from China.

B. Answers will vary.

page 9:
2. men   3. women
4. people   5. people
6. books   7. stories
8. families   9. countries
10. problems   11. classes

pages 10–11: Answers will vary.

pages 12–13: Answers given in story.

page 14: Answers will vary.

page 15:
2. c   3. b   4. a   5. c   6. b
7. a   8. a

Unit 2 ● ● ●

page 18: Answers will vary.

page 19: Answers will vary.

page 20:
2. speak   3. listen   4. read
stories   5. stay in one's seat
6. work with a group
7. work with a partner
8. work at a desk   9. ask a
question   10. laugh

page 21: Answers cannot be shown
here.

page 22: Answers will vary.

page 23:
A. 2. pay phones
3. library   4. vending
machine   5. cafeteria
6. stairs

B. Where is the cafeteria?
Where are the pay
phones?
Where are the vending
machines?
Where are the rest
rooms?

pages 24–25: Answers will vary.

pages 26–27: Answers will vary.

page 28: Answers will vary.

page 29:
2. a   3. b   4. c   5. a   6. c
7. a   8. c

Unit 3 ● ● ●

page 32: Answers will vary.

page 33:

A. sister, mother, son, grandmother, daughter, brother, grandfather, parents, children

B. Answers will vary.

page 34:

A. 3. on

B. 1. in   2. in   3. in   4. in

C. 1. in   2. in   3. in   4. in   5. on

page 35:

2. What is your last name?
   Aziz.
   Please spell it.
   A-Z-I-Z.
   OK, thanks.

3. What is your name?
   Peter Lee.
   Excuse me?
   Peter. Peter Lee.
   Nice to meet you Peter.

4. Where does your son live?
   I don't understand.
   Your son.
   Where does he live?
   Oh! In Haiti!

page 36: Answers will vary.

page 37:

3. Where do your friends live?

4. Where does (your friend, mother, sister, etc.) live?

5. Where do you live?

6. Where do your parents live?

pages 38–39: Answers will vary.

page 40: Answers will vary.

page 41: Answers will vary.

page 42:

2. 471-0132   Waldo Sanchez
3. 984-8608   Jay Sandelin
4. 988-3259   T. Sanchez-Martinez
5. 982-3139   Yvette Sanchez
6. 438-8514   J. Sander

page 43: 1. b   2. a   3. a   4. c   5. c
6. a   7. c   8. b

Unit 4 • • •

pages 46–47: Answers will vary.

page 48: 3. b   4. e   5. c   6. f   7. j
8. h   9. g   10. i

page 49: Answers will vary.

page 50: 2. makes   3. helps
4. finishes   5. paints

page 51:

3. When do you start work?
4. When do you finish work?
5. When do you eat dinner?
6. When do you go to bed?

page 52:

A. Tuesday, Wednesday, Thursday, Friday, Saturday, Sunday

B. Answers will vary.

page 53:

A. I leave my first job (at) 2 P.M. I pick up my son from school. When my wife gets home (at) 4:00, I go to my second job. Sometimes I work overtime (on) Saturday. (On) Sunday we go to the supermarket.

B. Answers will vary.

page 54:

2. from 12:00 to 8:00
3. from 10:00 to 4:00
4. from 9:00 to 6:00
5. Ramona and Lee
6. Lee and Inez

page 55:

1. from 1:00 P.M. to 11:00 P.M.
2. from noon to 2:00 A.M.
3. from 7:00 A.M. to 9:00 P.M.
4. from 7:00 A.M. to 5:00 P.M.
5. It's closed on Sunday.
6. from 7:00 A.M. to 6:00 P.M.

page 56:	A. 2. f 3. a 4. b 5. d 6. i 7. e 8. g 9. j 10. h
	B. Answers will vary.
page 57:	1. c 2. a 3. b 4. a 5. c 6. a 7. c 8. b

Unit 5 • • •

pages 60–61:	Answers will vary.
page 62:	A. 2. fish 3. apple 4. coffee 5. chicken 6. pizza 7. pears 8. carrots
	B. Answers will vary.
page 63:	Answers will vary.
pages 64–65:	A. 2. f 3. g 4. b 5. c 6. e 7. a
	B. 3. sixty-nine cents 4. five dollars 5. thirteen forty-nine 6. ten dollars 7. three forty-nine 8. six twenty-seven
page 66:	A. 2. $1.00 3. 98¢ 4. 19¢ 5. 98¢
	B. Answers will vary.
page 67:	A. Answers will vary.
	B. 2. supermarket 3. laundromat 4. bank 5. shoe store 6. health clinic 7. community center, park (or anywhere!) 8. park 9. police station
page 68:	2. Avelino is shopping at a supermarket. 3. Avelino and his friend are talking. 4. The men are playing dominoes, and Avelino is watching them.

page 69:	4. Yes, they are. 5. No, they aren't. 6. No, he isn't. 7. Yes, he is. 8. No, he isn't.
page 70:	A. 3. but 4. and
	B. Answers will vary.
page 71:	1. b 2. a 3. c 4. c 5. a 6. b 7. b 8. b

Unit 6 • • •

page 74:	A. 2. taught 3. had 4. gave 5. cooked 6. ate 7. danced 8. cried 9. showed 10. looked 11. listened 12. played 13. decorated 14. wore
	B. **Regular:** listened, cooked, cried, danced, showed, looked, listened, played, decorated **Irregular:** taught, had, gave, ate, wore
page 75:	C. 2. cooked 3. gave 4. showed 5. decorated 6. wore 7. ate 8. laughed 9. cried
	D. Answers will vary.
page 76:	Answers will vary.
page 77:	A. 3. on 4. in 5. on 6. in 7. on 8. on
	B. Answers will vary.
page 78:	A. FEBRU<u>AR</u>Y, <u>M</u>ARCH, <u>A</u>P<u>R</u>IL, M<u>AY</u>, <u>J</u>UNE, <u>J</u>U<u>L</u>Y, AUGU<u>ST</u>, <u>SE</u>PTEMB<u>ER</u>, OCTOB<u>ER</u>, N<u>OV</u>EMBER, DEC<u>EM</u>BER

page 78:
B. Jan. = January
Dec. = December
Sept. = September
Feb. = February
Apr. = April
Nov. = November
Aug. = August
Oct. = October

C. Answers will vary.

page 79:
A. 3. 8/2/94   4. 5/18/70
5. 7/4/96   6. 12/30/90
7. 3/1/95   8. 9/2/84

B. Answers will vary.

page 80: Answers will vary.

page 81:
2. Friday
3. Sunday
4. Wednesday
5. Friday
6. Tuesday

pages 82–83: Answers are in the story.

page 84:
1. b   2. a   3. b
4. b   5. a   6. b
7. c   8. a